ALPHABET BOOK

FOR MY PARENTS

TABLE OF CONTENTS

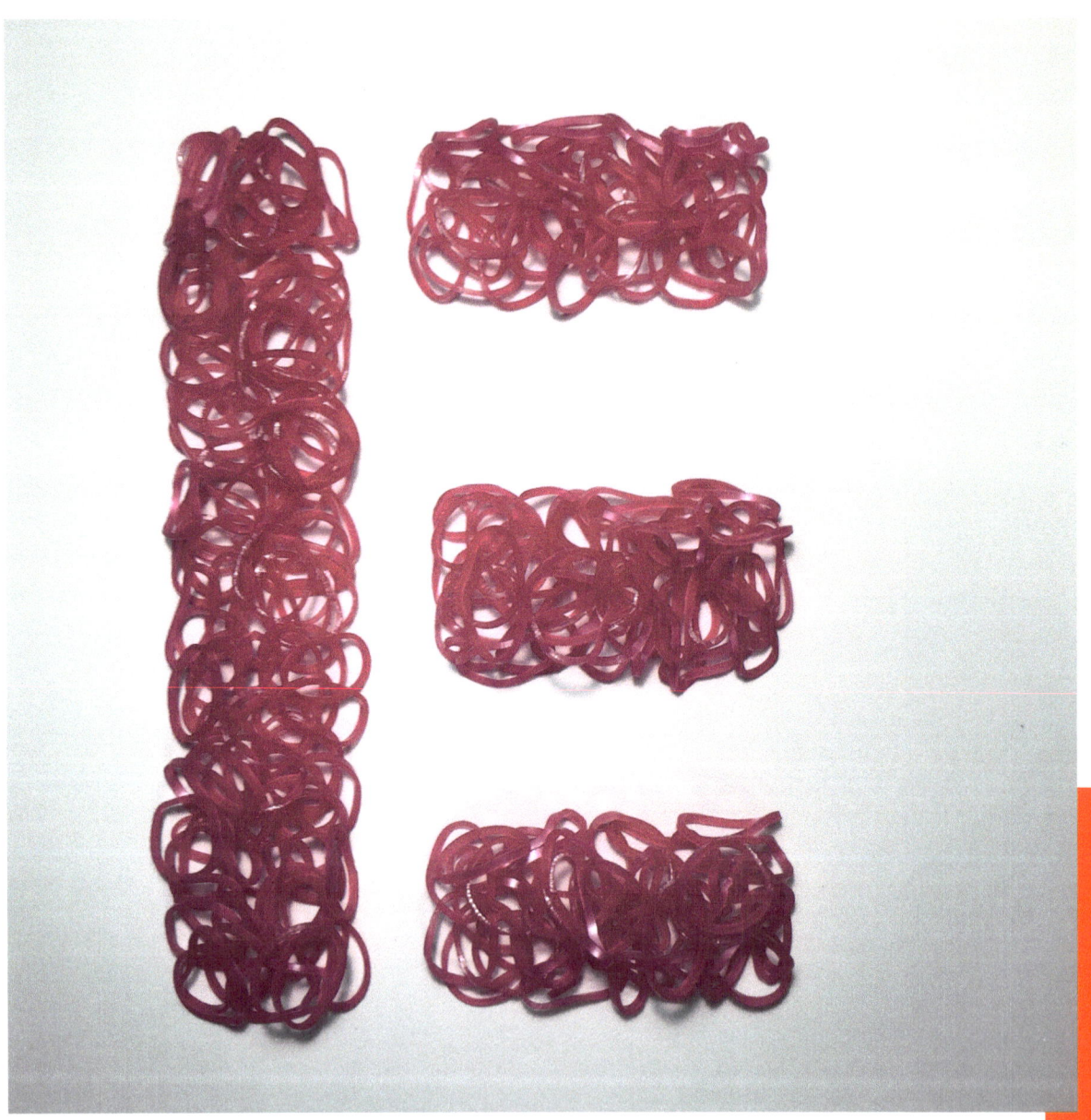

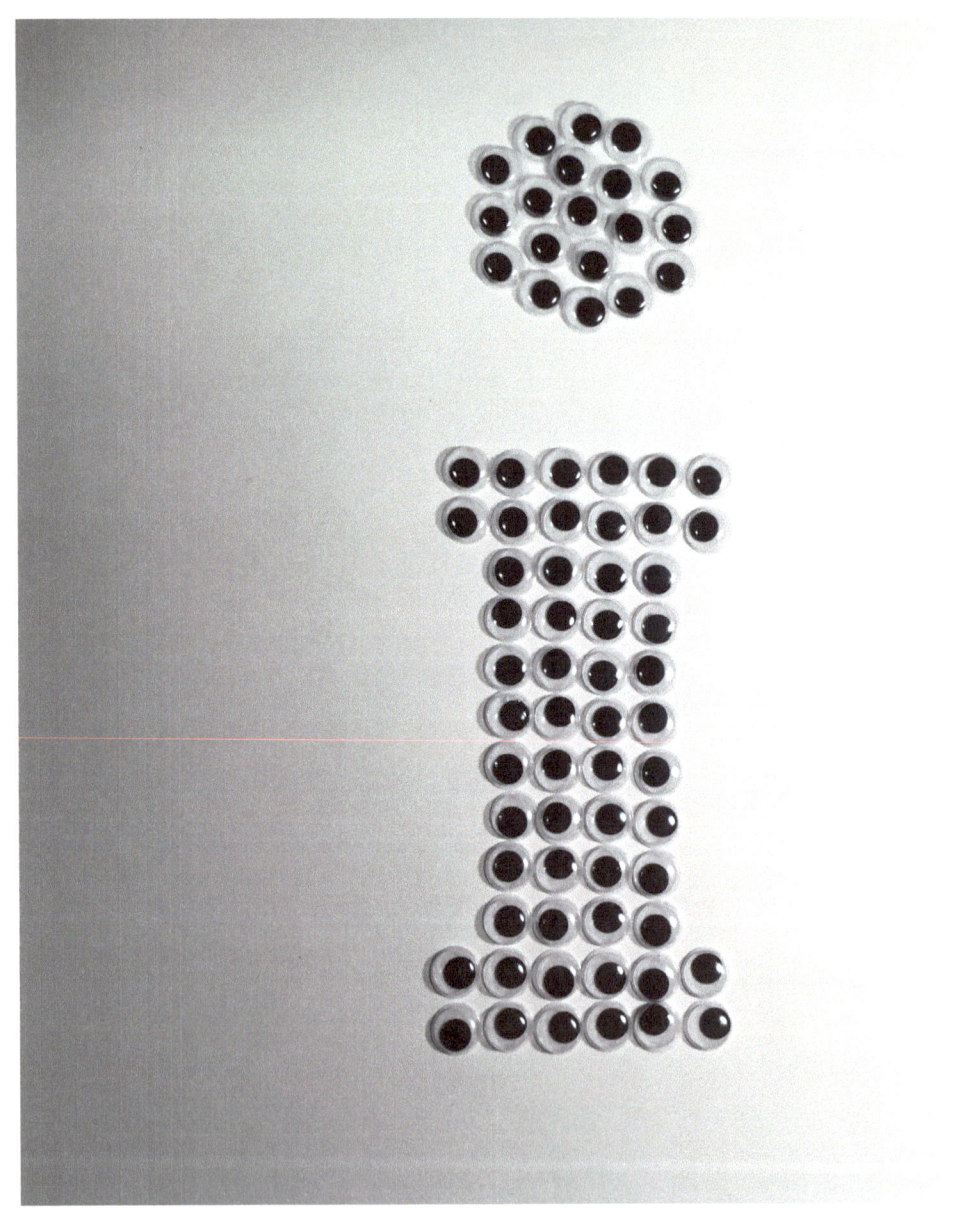

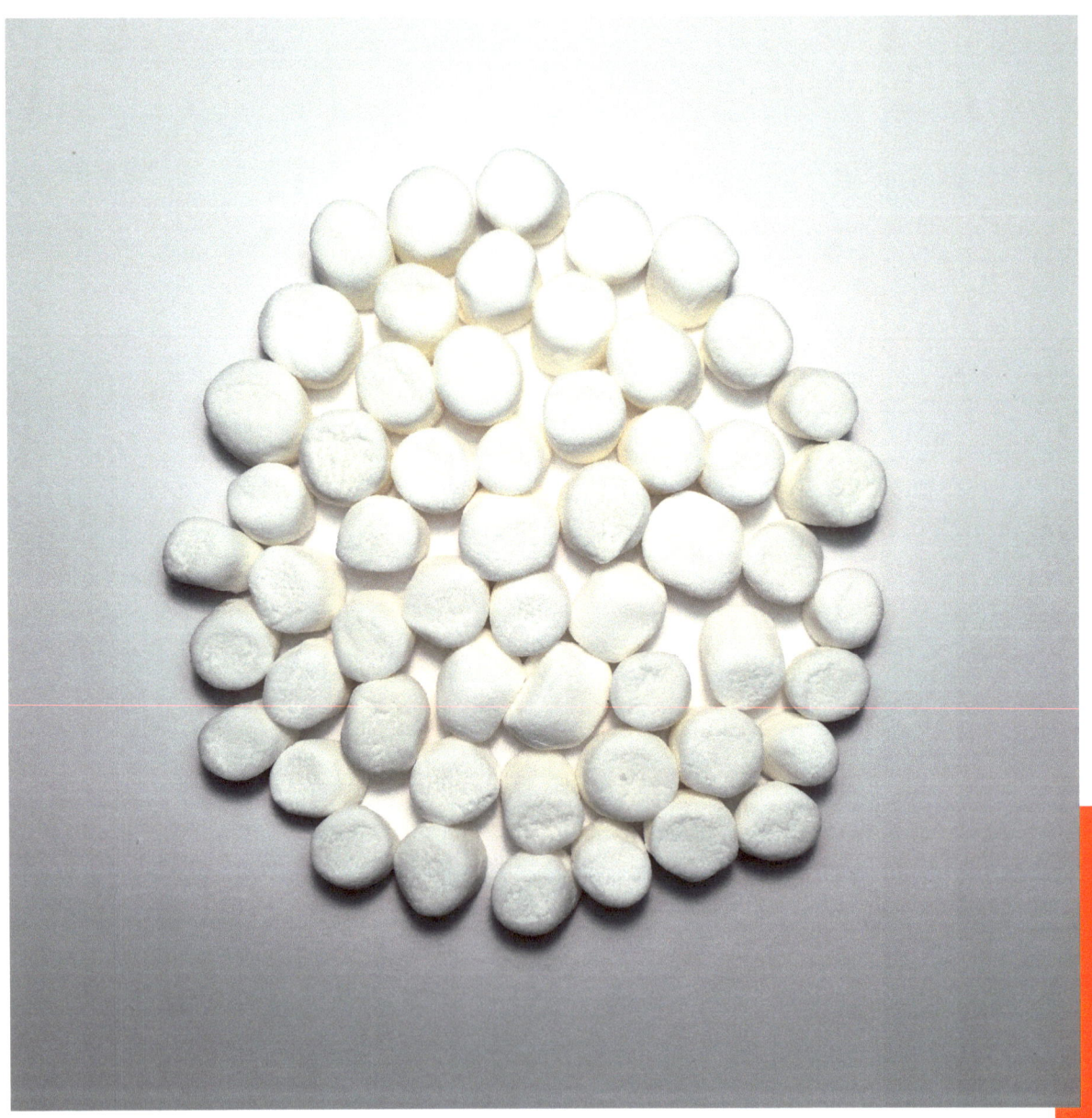

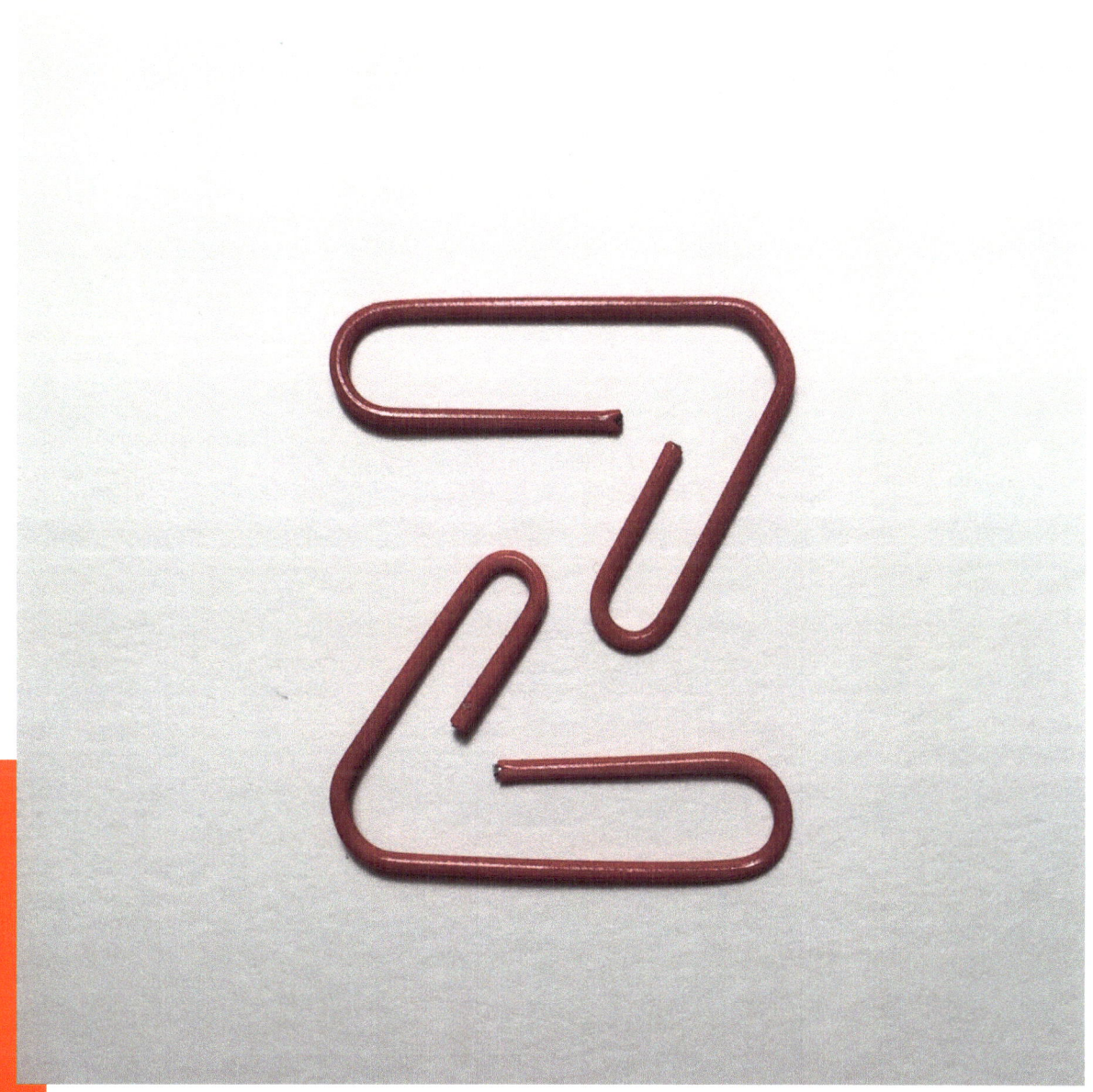

PART TWO

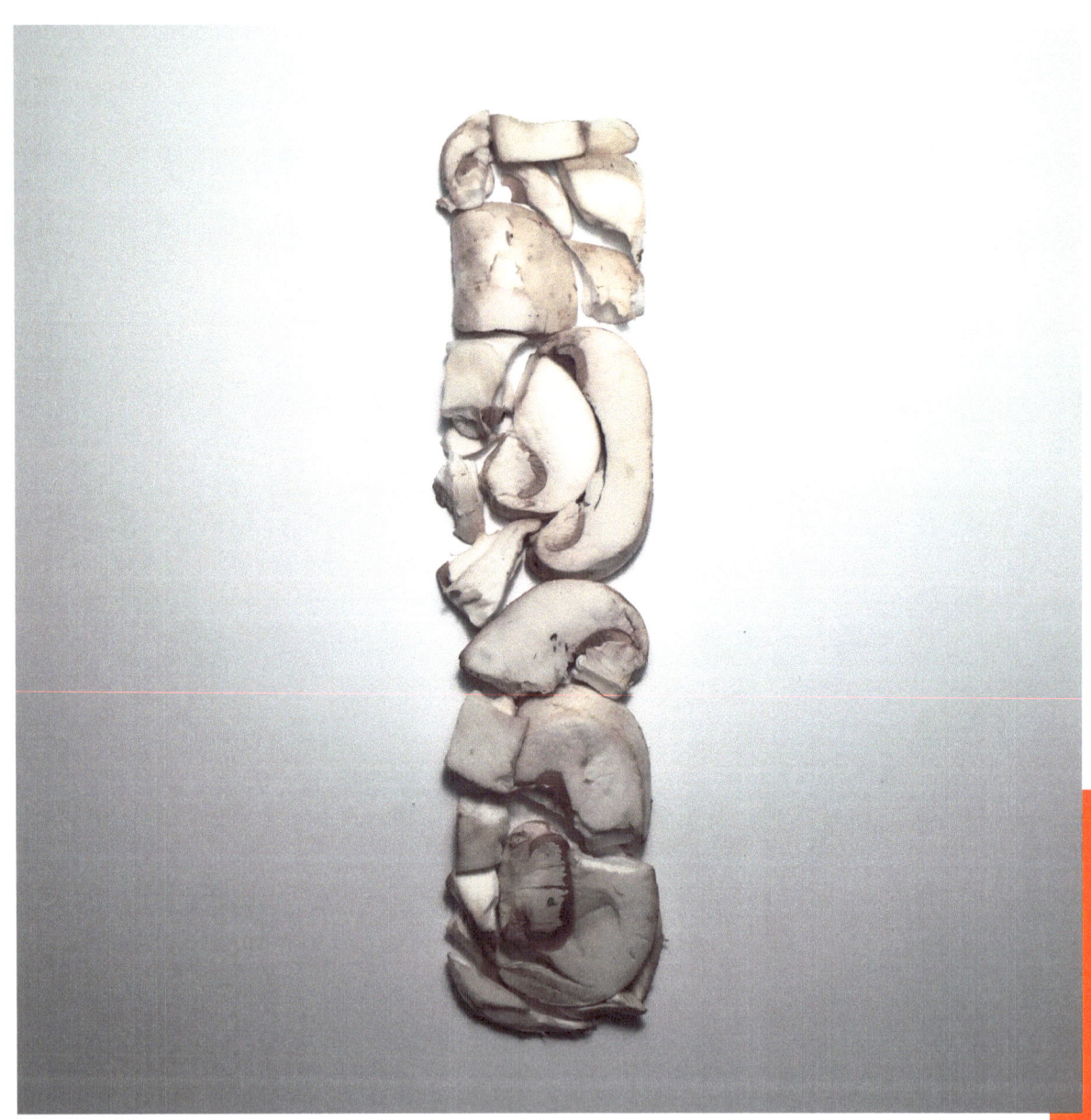

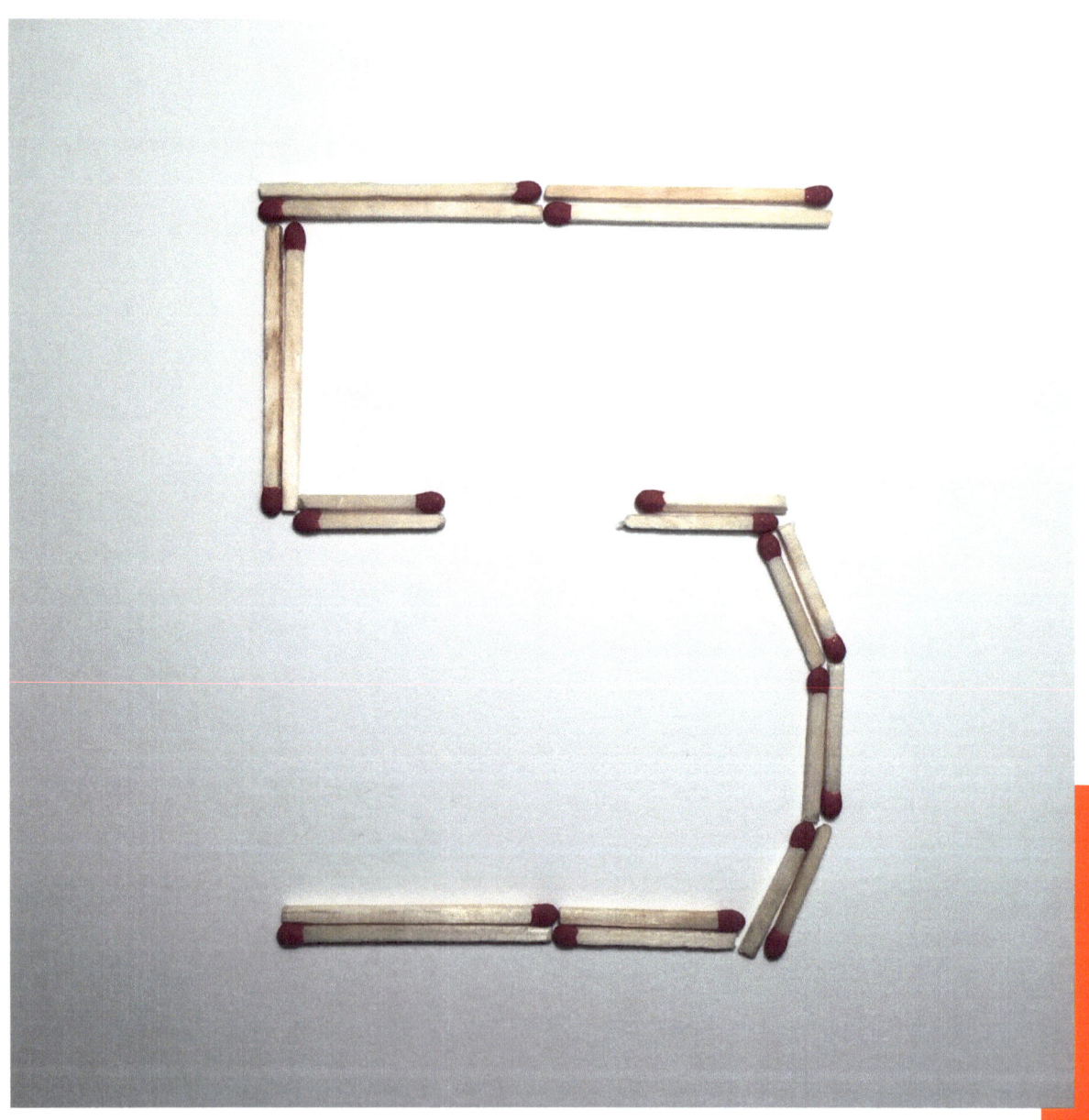

"MY ALPHABET
STARTS WITH THIS LETTER CALLED YUZZ.
IT'S THE LETTER I USE TO SPELL

YUZZ-A-MA-TUZZ

YOU'LL BE SORT OF SURPRISED

WHAT THERE IS TO BE FOUND

ONCE YOU GO BEYOND 'Z'

AND START POKING AROUND!"

-DR SEUSS

43

www.ingramcontent.com/pod-product-compliance
Lightning Source LLC
Chambersburg PA
CBHW060837290526
45792CB00006BB/1960